40 Days to a Joyful Motherhood

40 Days to a Joyful Motherhood

Devotions and Coloring Book to Nourish Mom

SARAH HUMPHREY

ABINGDON PRESS
NASHVILLE

40 DAYS TO A JOYFUL MOTHERHOOD
Devotions and Coloring Book to Nourish Mom

Copyright © 2016 by Sarah Humphrey

Library of Congress Cataloging-in-Publication Data has been requested.

ISBN 978-1-5018-3487-5

17 18 19 20 21 22 23—10 9 8 7 6 5 4 3 2

MANUFACTURED IN THE UNITED STATES OF AMERICA

Dedicated to my first loves: David, Ella, Micah, Lucy, and Oliver.

And to all the women in the world who rejoice in the title of "mom."

Contents

Welcome

Every mother can relate with one common theme during her pregnancy, childbirth, first days of parents and beyond—

The need for Joy.

What makes us most effective as birthers and nurturers, as boundary makers and guidance counselors, is joy. When we speak from a posture of abundance and life, we fill our surroundings with peace and purpose. When we live out of exhaustion, fear, and depression, we deplete the very place we are supposed to steward. As mothers, we face both of these situations at different times. It is inevitable. Motherhood is full of trial and error, leadership and development, unconditional love and mistakes. Yet, in the myriad of vast emotions and experiences, we can learn how to cultivate a home full of honor. As we face ourselves and hand ourselves over to Jesus to be healed, loved, and filled up, we can then create an environment where we give our families and friends the space to do the same.

What every mother wants is to be happy and healthy. What I've developed out of my own journey of motherhood is a tool just for that. Out of my ups and my downs, I'm learning how to pray. I'm also learning how to look at myself deeply, how to live life simply, and how to give practically. My hope through this project is that it might give you insight and tools on how to do the same in your own unique experience.

So bring your kids' crayon box or buy your own. Let's doodle and play as only moms can!

Let joy be our portion!

Foreword

David Humphrey

A foreword is typically a short introduction of a book, written by someone other than the primary author. It is important to have this. You see, the writer of any foreword usually knows the author and can vouch for his or her credibility on the subject matter that is neatly crafted and awaiting for you on the subsequent pages. It is one person's way to say, "Hey everybody, you should read this! It's going to be huge, monumental, and—dare I say?—life-changing. And I know this to be true because I actually *know* this person. What this person says is from her heart, and you can trust it." Every good book with a strong message should have a foreword, especially if you want the book to be credible.

And in this case it is a little different. Not only do I know this person, I am married to her. How's that for credibility?

40 Days to a Joyful Motherhood is a journey on motherhood. On the outer appearance, it looks and feels like a devotional that you can walk through yourself, get comfy with, and partake in while on your own journey. And it is. Yet underneath, it comes from a place where the good, the bad, and the messy have surfaced; the sweat, the stains, and the tears of sorry and even gladness are present; the breakthroughs, the overcoming, the small victories are won. It is a place where all moms can relate.

As a dad and as a husband, I recognize that God has wired me a certain way to provide for my family. To be the steady, wise, and strong voice. To be the leader who keeps our family compass heading north—with my crew in line and ready to go into the battles of life, no matter how bright or challenging it may be. Ready, prepared, and confident. I am here to kiss scraped knees, bumps, and bruises and to give assurance and encouragement. I am also here to be present—with my time and with my support.

But I also see that as a dad and husband, I'm highly flawed and ill-equipped to complete the job. I lack certain qualities that only a mom and wife can provide. And I am so thankful that Sarah is very equipped to complete the job for our family. Not only has God wired her with certain attributes that make her gentle, warm, and approachable for each of our children, she is in the thick of it daily. She lives it. So it is not only in her DNA, but she has gone through the basic training and is now on the front lines. She has not won all the battles of motherhood (yet), but she is sweeping through it capturing small victories at a time. You can say that there is a lot of "pressing through" in our house.

When I sit back and watch Sarah do something that only a mother knows how to do for our Ella, Lucy, and Oliver, I know she did not learn these things from any one book, blog, or conversation from another mom at a park. But I know she does these things from a place of her own surrendering, a place where she has learned to be present with each of her own children and where they are in that moment of that day.

From new moms to soon-to-be empty nesters, this is a journey for you. Dads and husbands throughout the world know that God has wired you all special. We cannot make up or fake our way through the life and ways you provide. There is an authenticity that cannot be mimicked or copied. We are with you and cheer you on as you do the things only mothers can do. So as you journey through these pages, be sure to take time to reflect, find balance and inner healing, and marvel on the goodness of God. Also know that, along with many other women who are most likely experiencing the same motherhood triumphs and tribulations that you are on this very day, you can also find rest here—at least for a few moments before your child comes strolling in asking for homework help.

Introduction

Sarah Humphrey

Let's talk about the perfect, but sometimes does not feel so perfect, *storm*.

Hormones. No sleep. Body parts that are all kinds of sizes they weren't before. Skin that's flabby and swollen and creating muffin tops that make the world go round.

Emotions of love and joy and excitement and "Oh God, please don't cry again."

And if you are blessed, older siblings who do not understand how your body and personhood just went through a hurricane and is somehow holding on with one thread of dignity and a side of hemorrhoid cream.

Yeah, I said it.

Welcome to childbirth and motherhood. And in just a few short days, you will have no idea where all that milk came from and wonder how your body became the creative source to keep a human being alive.

It is amazing really, and it is full of curiosity and expectation and learning and growing.

It is also full of what feels like "not enough time." Not enough time is really just a shift of priorities even though it doesn't always feel like that in the moment.

My biggest shift in parenting bliss was learning how to process well. In the midst of trying to live a daily life, moms are constantly trying to listen, troubleshoot, respond to needs, and do all of the above without many avenues for self-care. And this, in fact, is the most crucial time in life for self-care, not just as a person but for the role of motherhood.

When I decided to be a stay-at-home mom, my greatest asset was using motherhood as a time to learn to nurture. Not only as a mother but also for myself. Bringing a baby into the world is a season of bringing new creativity, new life, and new gifts to the world.

It is also a time of relearning and regrowing; it is a time of exposure. It is a season where many of the unnurtured parts of us start to show up quite loudly, and so it is also a time of healing and repair.

The tricky part is there is not much personal time. A newborn is a bit of a presence hog, and if there are other children involved, personal time really is limited. What I learned to do, and am still learning to do, is make the most of the time I do have for myself. I had to shift priorities and learn how to manage all the emotions and inspiration and creativity of my being—and then funnel them into something productive and life-giving to me. I had to give myself time for release. Because if I did not give myself room for creative release, I would end up spewing out that middle-of-the-road processing onto someone else—which is usually hurried, frustrating, and potentially hurtful.

I am not usually a formula type person; I am more of a go-with-the-flow type person, but sometimes my flow ends up creating a pattern. Ironically, that pattern gives me wisdom on how to do well the next time. In hopes that my pattern might be encouraging to you, here is my motherhood story!

Identity for Mamahood

My husband works for a best-selling book publisher, and he says the books that sell the quickest off the shelves are the ones with the most blunt of titles. In other words: *5 Steps to Be Happy* or *How to Deal with Anxiety* or *Hi, I Just Had Three Kids and Am Trying to Make Sense of My Crazy Self.* You get the idea.

So when it came to having kids and naming them, I first went with what sounded good (because I love beautiful names), but I also went with what had deep meaning to us as a married couple. And simply enough, the names of my kids have helped me give purpose to their everyday activities and my everyday interactions with them. In other words, I knew what each child represented to me. And by knowing that, I had wisdom for how to give myself grace and truth while walking through not only this particular season with them but hopefully their entire lives.

Our Ella is the female version of "Who Is Like God?" She teaches me how to listen and how to move. Our Lucy is "Light." She teaches me about self-care and healthy boundaries. Our Oliver is "Peace and Fruitfulness." He teaches me to regain laughter and strength.

Sometimes it's easy to think of each child as a book (we are all the authors of our stories, yes?), and their names are the blunt title I remind myself of when I'm trying to figure out how to raise them as well as grow personally.

If I have clung to one thing during this season of life, it has been to move toward what their names and their identities mean to me. Children are God's gifts to us; so my personal "gifts" are God's representation of women, His light, and His peace. These are my keys. When all else seems overwhelming with dirty diapers and crying and temper tantrums, I go back to these keys. These are the purposes that God is having me steward in myself, in my marriage, and in each one of them. These are the gifts that have been given as a result of love between David and me; this is who we are as a family and what we value. When I can see the big picture, it is easier to let the small and overly complicated details work themselves out. Because you know as moms, we obsess over the details while we are parenting ALL THE TIME. "Is my kid nursing well? Is my kid going to learn how to talk? Is my kid eating enough healthy food? Is my kid sleeping through the night?" And on and on and on. And it is the details that start to kill our energy and our joy and our peace. The details start making us compare ourselves to one another and start mommy wars. The details make us perfectionists who are hard on ourselves for every small, minute issue that goes awry (which happens MORE when that's what we are focusing on).

So, instead, I chose to move toward *meaning,* which gave me the wisdom to sort out the details well. I chose to focus on identity. I decided to move toward God's beauty for women, His light, and His peace, because those are our kids. As I focused on this, the opposites showed up often (because there is an opponent for every good choice), but *I knew my goal.* So, as the opposites reared their ugly head, I just reminded myself of what I had birthed. Those beautiful human beings with those identities came out of my womb. I decided I was going to continue moving toward their God-given design with all my might while also honoring the challenges and feelings that surfaced in my heart until they were dealt with completely. And this was quite a number of cycles, and still can be. But people are onions: we have a lot of layers. We have unresolved hurts, experiences, and generational lines of the same types of experiences that have mixed their way into our DNA—and it can take a lot of focus and hard work to rewire ourselves.

But in all reality, the opposite feelings or meanings of their names (like hatred or misuse of women, or darkness, or anxiety) do not belong to their identities or to me. Those mishaps in my generational or personal wiring just became *obvious* to me when their true identities were born and as I tried to steward their lives well in daily happenings. Those mishaps just showed me where to close the gaps, so I could be happier and more effective as a person and wife and mother.

My first round of encouragement to the mamas of today is this: find out what your kids' names mean. Sit down and ask yourself what they represent to you. And when the opposite of that starts to reveal itself (because it will), face it eye-to-eye. Honor the emotions that the opposition brings up, and keep moving toward the prize.

Because as we move toward the prize, our faith ripens and our fears disappear. And what our children need most from us as mothers is *joy.*

Rejoice always. Pray continually. Give thanks in every situation because that is God's will for you in Christ Jesus. 1 Thessalonians 5:16-18

Day 1

I will make of you a great nation and will bless you.
I will make your name respected, and you will be a blessing.
Genesis 12:2

As we embark on the journey of motherhood, remember our identity as a person is of utmost significance. We can't give with sustenance unless we are nourished to our core. Today is about us. Who are you? What is your name? What is the meaning of your name? Who you are is important, and it is vital to your success as a person, as a wife, as a mother, and as a friend. Often times, we put ourselves on the back burner when we realize that our children need our attention twenty-four hours of the day and seven days of the week. In the midst of the needs, our greatest asset knows who we are. Today is a day to remember.

Let's focus on our names. Write down your full name. If you don't know the meaning of your name, Google it. Find out why you were given your particular name. Listen to your birth story. Invite yourself into recalibrating all the life experiences, good and bad, that makes up you and your life. This is a time of rebirth. Even as you have birthed a child, you are also birthing a new version of yourself!

A Simple Prayer

Jesus, let me learn more about who I am. I open my heart to hear
You speak into the identity You have created for me.

Hello! My name is...

Day 2

Adorn yourself with splendor and majesty;
clothe yourself with honor and esteem.
Job 40:10

What fills your love tank? How do you refuel? Think big or small, simple or complex. Acts of self-care and self-love are extremely important to mothers. Filling-up before giving-out is essential to living life well and giving with excellence. What we fail to give ourselves, we fail to release to others.

Before I was a mother, I had an extreme addiction to giving out of order. I am a giver by nature and love to help others, but without understanding boundaries in a proper context, it was easy for me to serve more than my mind and body could handle. When I became a mother, it forced me to look at myself. It helped me look at the way I thought, ate, and exercised as well as the way I spent my time and energy. It rewired my whole system of doing things in every way imaginable. It saved my life in many ways.

The transition to motherhood is very abrupt as a baby takes up every hour of every day (and night). And so, with this new life, I learned how to take cover and take care. I learned how to set healthy limits and how to open myself to God's love, self-love, and friends who cared. I reminded myself of joy with simple things and big things: a cup of coffee, an hour of quiet, a trip with girlfriends, and also with journaling and coloring. What I wanted to do on a regular basis was to be kind to myself.

Find ways today to look for simple joys. Come back to this entry later and write down a few of the kind things you did for yourself today. Spend time looking at your actions today and how you took care of yourself.

A Simple Prayer

Jesus, help me to fill my love tank first. Please give me practical
tips on how to take good care of myself.

Adorn yourself with splendor & majesty; clothe yourself with honor and esteem.

Job 40:10

Day 3

Anyone who needs wisdom should ask God, whose very nature is to give
to everyone without a second thought, without keeping score. Wisdom will
certainly be given to those who ask.
James 1:5

Becoming self-aware is one of our greatest personal tools. Recognizing areas where we struggle or where we overextend ourselves are the keys to creating proper balance and boundaries in our lives. After we create an environment of self-care, it is good to watch ourselves for where we get off kilter, overemotional, or irritated. These are signals to us to listen to ourselves, to let go of difficult emotions, and to choose a revised path. When I feel depleted or anxious, I realize that I have inside work to do. A struggle is actually the path to greatness. Whether it is lack of sleep, my child's health, or any other experience in life, I can face any difficulty by self-awareness, releasing toxicity, setting a good boundary, and re-creating joy.

The best way to come to a higher version of ourselves is to release toxicity in our lives. Sometimes that is putting a boundary on a relationship, on extra activities, or on other stressors that create an environment that fails to thrive. When we give ourselves space to be the best version of ourselves, we can let go of the things that hinder us.

What are some boundaries in your life that need to be drawn? What are some toxins you would like to release? What are some emotions that you need to process through and let go?

A Simple Prayer

Jesus, help me to become self-aware. Please give me wisdom and
guidance to know my boundaries and to be honest with my emotions.

Day 4

On the day I cried out, you answered me.
You encouraged me with inner strength.
Psalm 138:3

After we've brought ourselves into a posture of peace and joy, we can then give from an outflow to our family. Just as we need to be reminded of our own identity, so do our loved ones. If you are married, what is the name of your husband? What does it mean? What are the names of your children? What do those names mean?

It is important to find the meaning of their names because this will show us how to encourage them, build them up, and feed them with the best soul food. As mothers, we call our family *up* to their identity, and we put boundaries on what hinders that identity. When we recognize the opposite spirit rising against who they are, we remind them of truth. This is always the key. We never want to shame or point blame; we always want to call them higher, release nurture, and then set a guideline for better behavior.

We are better wives when we call our husbands up to their potential instead of nag about their weaknesses. We steward greatness, safety, and peace in our children when we give out both encouragement and wisdom.

Moms are often most vulnerable to imbalance because of the many demands on their time and resources. When we speak from a place of identity in ourselves to a place of identity in our loved ones, we create balance for our family to thrive.

Write down the meaning behind the names of your husband and children. Also, write down the opposites of their names so that you are aware of what they might need to overcome obstacles in their lives.

A Simple Prayer

Jesus, please help me to encourage the identity and potential in those
I love. Give me eyes to see them the way You see them.

Day 5

Do not conform to the pattern of this world, but be transformed
by the renewing of your mind. Then you will be able to test and approve
what God's will is—his good, pleasing and perfect will.
Romans 12:2 NIV

Transformation is the key to living a joyful life. When we are able to recognize and interrupt broken patterns in our lives and in the lives of our children, we learn the essence of forgiveness. And in forgiveness, we learn the proper way to steward. I want to steward joy in my home. In order to do that, I realize a few practical steps go a long way.

I honor original design. God says He created us, and we are good. This is my standard for identity. It is also obvious that I have and will, at times, fall short of this original design. Out of His good grace, God gave me Jesus. It is in this place of surrender, humility, and brokenness that I can receive God's grace. When I have given Him those weak and fragile parts, the mistakes and the failures, the bad behavior and the sin, I experience His gift toward me. In the gift of Jesus, I am filled with the joy and peace to start making better decisions. And with my good decisions comes transformation.

This transformation gives me strength for myself, and it releases the essence of true motherhood through me. Good mothers honor design, they understand sin, they ask for forgiveness, they fill up with joy, and they make better decisions for the future. We all begin here, and it is never too late to start on this path. Whether you are a mother to be, a new mother, or have been a mother for a long time, we rely on this cycle. Transformation is the beauty of life. Understanding and promoting this cycle is what makes us mothers.

Think about what you shared on Day 1 as the meaning of your name; this is your original design. Day 2 shared ways you can help honor that design. Day 3 discussed ways that we have fallen short or areas we need healing. Day 4 is who we primarily share that healing with. Today, let's ask for transformation in this cycle. In essence, ask for a Day 3½. Thank God for goodness and for who you are, and acknowledge where you need to go. Apologize for where you went wrong, and offer up a healing transformation so that you can give well to yourself and to your family. Take some time to pray and be with God inside this cycle.

A Simple Prayer

Jesus, transform me. Please give me the tools to steward my life
and the life of my children in a meaningful and joyful way.

Do NOT conform to the patterns of this world but be transformed by the renewing of your mind...

Romans 12:2

Expectations, Pain, Hopes, and Dreams

The greatest gift in my life as a person, a wife, a mother, and a friend is intercession. C. S. Lewis says, "Pain insists upon being attended to. God whispers to us in our pleasures, speaks in our consciences, but shouts in our pains. It is his megaphone to rouse a deaf world." As a human being, it is inevitable; you know pain.

If you have ever birthed a child, you know pain. If you have ever carried a friend's burden, you know pain. If you have ever had a loved one pass from this life, you know pain. If you have ever really lived, you know pain.

Pain is often part of our lives. Not always, but often. And, unfortunately, many of us have not been given many tools to understand pain. We find myriad "treatments" to numb it, pill pop it, pass by it, or drink it down. This is a detriment to our culture, our children, our families, and to our livelihood.

Since my oldest, Ella, was born, I have been on a journey to express trapped pain in my body. Because of my sensitive nature, I have a predisposition to absorb every environment I walk into. Not only did I have my own life experiences and traumas to work through, but I also carried the experiences and traumas of others that I encountered. Some call it empathy, some call it hypersensitivity, some call it prophetic intercession, and some call it psychic abilities. What it is for sure is absorption, and many people are wired this way, especially women.

What I learned after Ella was born was that I needed outlets to release all of the absorbed energies my body was manifesting. I started having health issues: thyroid problems, kidney stones, and nervous exhaustion, among others. It was the beginning stages of the birthing of my life's real voice. As I gave birth with each child that came into my womb and left, I was filled with more and more energy to disperse. But before it turned into positive energy, it showed up as anxiety. When I was touched by new life, I was more and more inspired. And the more inspired I became, the more I needed release. Without the release, the emotions I had tapped into would cause me to grow toxic inside. And that was and is always my cue to create.

When inspiration strikes and emotions are triggered, it is the perfect time for processing. And often times, it is the process of pain (can I say childbirth?) that propels us into real life.

Today, with our ability to communicate with others instantly (social media) as well as the great opportunity for freedom of expression, many people feel the need for immediate release. A problem with this type of release is that many people do not process their pain before they express their voice, and it can actually trigger more harmful results.

This issue has propelled the mommy wars, the vaccination and formula fights, the political mumbo jumbo, and all the childish behavior that is overtly overtaking our forms of communication. In reality, we have great tools to make a difference in the lives of others. Instead it often feels like stones are being thrown everywhere. In my opinion, we need to laugh more! We need more things to be joyful about, and that means we need to be intentional about our personal processes.

What I have learned as I have processed my own pain is this: It takes inside work to have outside results. If we are inspired and/or triggered by something, whether it is online or with our spouses or kids or job, it is a gift. It might not always seem like a gift at the time (because sometimes inspiration requires change), but it is. It is an opportunity to awaken, to look inside and find out what needs expressed. If we are inspired by something we find joyful, this is usually easy. If we are awakened by something that triggers our pain or insecurities, it can be a bit more work. In this case, our first response is often the blame game. The blame game is actually the *worst* possible result for a triggered emotion. If we want to influence anyone or anything, it always starts with inside work. If we need to bring correction or perspective to a situation, it starts with inside work. So many of our attempts at expressing ourselves have become swords to chop each other into pieces. And when this happens, we have dug our own grave. There is little planted correction in the tone of an impure voice.

The power in freedom of expression is humility, surrender, and validation. We are each trying to fill gaps in our family and society in some form, I hope. But in order to fill each other's gaps, we start with our own. This is why I love prayer! When I learn how to submit myself in prayer, I receive the grace I need to close my gap. When my gap is filled, I have excess grace to give someone else. This excess grace can then be translated in conversation and transformation (even when that conversation is a difficult one). The most wonderful part of this process is after emotional pain has been released, control and fear are thrown out the window. When we are done trying to control one another's behavior, we are actually free to love one another. And it is in this place of respect that we can make healthy movement forward.

The interesting part of this process is that everyone is in her own unique storyline. This means that my path might not look like another person's path. I am working on closing my own gap. I am not comparing my gap to someone else's, and I am also not trying to fix anyone else's gap. If I work on the inside, from a place of humility (because I have baggage as much as anyone else), I do not feel a need to judge anyone else's situation. When I am free from judgment, I have the perfect platform to share my perspective. When I have shared my perspective, it may bring a course correction. And if so, that is *real life*! Then I have contributed in a healthy way; I have helped carry a burden; I have helped cover a wound; I have interceded; I have been part of a solution. This is how we transform harmful pain into productive pain. Once we have mastered this, we start to build muscle—and this muscle can be used to support many others, especially our children.

Day 6

"For I know the plans I have for you," declares the LORD, *"plans to prosper you and not to harm you, plans to give you hope and a future."*
Jeremiah 29:11 NIV

It is easy to celebrate life when God exceeds our expectations. Sometimes we hold really high expectations in an effort to keep ourselves safe from failure or loss of control. Other times we keep low expectations because we have been disappointed and are scared to hope. And sometimes our expectations are simply just ideas, perhaps what we would like to happen. We might not hold on too tightly or loosely, but they are guides for us. No matter the way we "expect," motherhood comes with hopes and dreams, pain and plans. When our expectations are exceeded or met, we often feel a sense of satisfaction or connection with life, our surroundings, and others. If our expectations are not met or are dramatically different, sometimes it takes some time to emotionally absorb the differences. Motherhood is an array of expectations, and we cannot predict very much of it. What we can do is learn how to process those expectations into a funnel that can be molded and shaped for the release God intends for us.

What expectations did you have of motherhood before becoming a mother? What are some of your expectations now? What are some of your hopes, dreams, and plans as a person? What are some of your hopes, dreams, and plans as a mother?

A Simple Prayer

Jesus, help me to celebrate when You have exceeded my expectations.
Guide my expectations of motherhood into a healthy funnel for release.

Day 7

I give thanks to you with all my heart, Lord.
I sing your praise before all other gods.
I bow toward your holy temple
and thank your name
for your loyal love and faithfulness
because you have made your name and word
greater than everything else.
On the day I cried out, you answered me.
You encouraged me with inner strength.
Psalm 138:1-3

When our expectations have been met with grace and excitement, we feel full. We feel like all is right with the world, and we are postured in a place of celebration. We meet our day with joy, and the world is our oyster. We exhibit gratitude from the very fiber of our beings. When our expectations come true, it is important to take note and give thanks. Gratitude heals our minds and bodies of hope deferred, of disappointment, and of depression. Giving thanks not only releases praise but it also shifts the mood of our home and environments. I want to spend my life being grateful for how I have been blessed. I want to give praise where I have seen God provide for me, where I have seen dreams come true, and where I have seen faithfulness. Giving thanks is a simple gesture that moves mountains. When I remember how to be grateful, I open myself up to the possibility of even more blessings.

What are some of the ways your expectations of motherhood have been met or exceedingly met? What are some of the simple joys in your life for which you can give thanks? Think big and small. Keep an ongoing journal or list of things that you are thankful for. You can always go back to this list when in need of a reminder, and you can watch it grow as you continue to give credit for blessings.

A Simple Prayer

Jesus, thank You for my life's simple joys. Thank You for continually blessing me. Remind me to stay alive in gratitude.

Gratitude

I am Thankful For...

Day 8

And we know that in all things God works for the good of those who love him,
who have been called according to his purpose.
Romans 8:28 NIV

Sometimes we hold expectations so high or make them so lofty that they are extremely difficult to attain, especially if they deal with another human being. One of the most wonderful things about God is that He is better than any expectation. He will always come through, always be faithful, and always be kind. Sometimes He positions us in a way that our human expectations fail so that He can fill us with the truth and the goodness of who He is. And in that, every expectation we could ever have is met.

The reality, though, is that we often have expectations in a human realm that sometimes are not met the way we had hoped. And when that happens, we work through disappointment. This is where we learn the art of grief. When we hope for something, and the seemingly opposite happens or our expectations for a situation are not met, there is a time for release. It is important to note these instances as they often repeat in cycles over our lives. It is important to be honest and grieve over what we hoped would happen that did not, and it is also important to place those expectations into God's hands so we can give Him space to perfectly heal us and weave His plan into action.

What are some areas as a person and as a mother where your expectations have not been met? What were some things you were looking forward to that turned out differently than you expected? What are a few disappointments that have developed in the midst of learning how to hope?

A Simple Prayer

Jesus, help me not to be stilted by expectations that turned out differently than I had hoped. Help me to give You my disappointments in exchange for true fulfillment.

Day 9

*Yes, goodness and faithful love
will pursue me all the days of my life,
and I will live in the Lord's house
as long as I live.
Psalm 23:6*

After we start to understand cycles in our lives where our expectations seem to be unmet and then grieve in response, we open ourselves up to other possibilities. When we make this sacred space in our heart to be honest with ourselves and to be honest with God, we can learn how to take ownership in our healing, admit our mistakes, and release any negative emotions that have been hindering our progress. We can also start to choose new patterns for our lives; we can create new strategies.

My personal preference to success is slow and steady. If I can make simple changes, one step at a time, I continually see improvement. A willing spirit combined with simple and practical changes can shift unmet expectations into a tree of life.

What are some simple ways to help rewire your expectations? How can you change habits that have been hindering you? How can you incorporate fifteen minutes a day of quiet and prayer into your life? Is there a safe friend or two you can ask for support in your journey?

A Simple Prayer

*Jesus, please give me the grace to grieve in response to unmet expectations.
Help me to find quiet time to pray daily and create new patterns for my life.*

Day 10

Let your gentleness show in your treatment of all people.
The LORD is near.
Philippians 4:5

After we decide how to start simply moving in the right direction, it is also important to make proper boundaries to that which hinders us. Sometimes we have to leave behind old triggers or toxic relationships if we are to bloom with grace. Other times, we just need to let go of old patterns. When we start moving forward with focus and clarity, with our expectations fully set on God, we have the strength to let go of hindrances. When we find purpose, we can let go of what entangles us, whether through repetitive practice or from simply choosing to ignore the old and build the new.

This is the season where we learn the art of gentleness, being kind to ourselves as we shift patterns and learn new ways to hope and dream. Motherhood comes with many surprises, and sometimes the key to success is simply being open with what is presented to us. Though children do not come with owner's manuals, we can listen to the Holy Spirit for guidance. We can pray, and we can become quiet in our souls. We can respond to God's leading in order to let go of where we are hindered. God's plans for us are always better than we could have expected or dreamed for ourselves. Our position is childlike faith, letting go of false beliefs, and moving toward His perfect heart for us.

What are some areas where you want to see freedom in your life? What are some hindrances that you want to let go? What are some simple ways you can promote self-care and gentleness in your day as you transition from hope-deferred into the Tree of Life?

A Simple Prayer

Jesus, help me to move in the right direction and create the proper boundaries for myself.
Please help me to learn the art of gentleness so that I can guide
my children with the wisdom of the Holy Spirit.

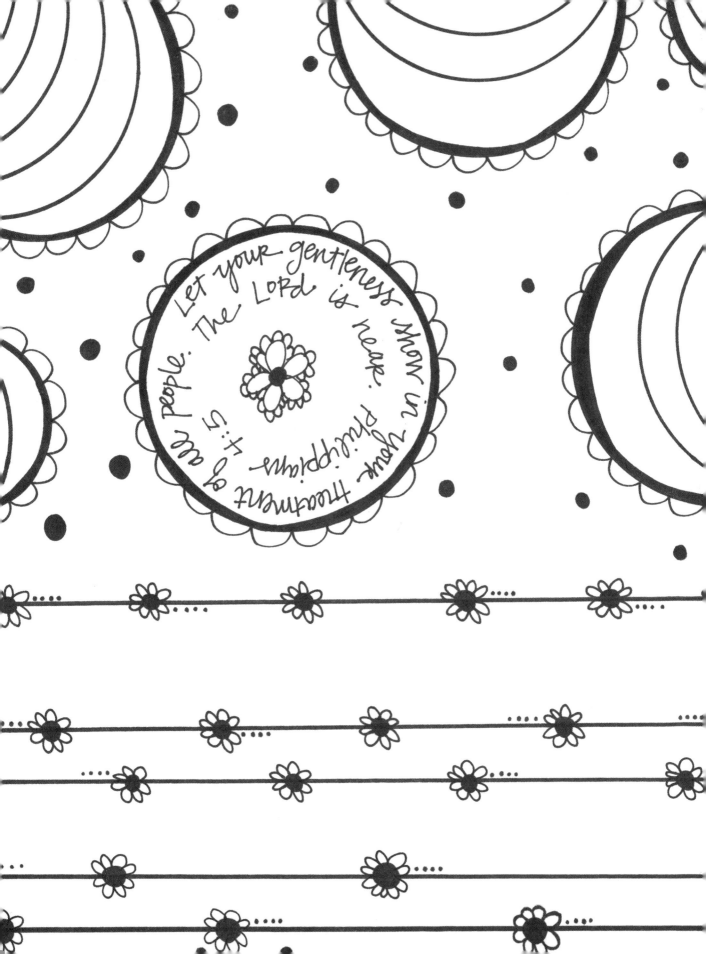

Let your gentleness show in your treatment of all people. The LORD is near. Philippians 4:5

Releasing Grief and Receiving New Life

I found this poetic story in one of my journals months after I had written it. It reminds me of how important it is to catalog my thoughts each day because I never know what I really write until I come back to it in the future. What an authentic picture of forgiveness and creativity; I did not even know its beauty was hanging around in my back pocket to share. Sometimes we fill up with strength and inspiration so that it gives us the courage and the patience to walk through the process. Mothers live lives full of patience and forgiveness. It can make us bitter, or it can make us come alive.

It's our choice. *Our children are such gifts.*

There's nothing like soaking in meditation and the sounds of God worship, only to then be released into a garment of child whines, demands, and tears.

What we soak in some moments gives us strength for the next wave.
We ebb and flow.

Breathe in Peace so we can exhale Life.

And when the chatter of surroundings competes with the peace of my new heart—
We make orange Jell-O.

When the boiling water bubbles and steams—and I have to tell the kids to "Step back. Do not get burned"—

I breathe.

I exhale dust.

And when they are pushing and shoving to see the gelatin melt just as I pour in the cup of cold water,

I breathe.

And when they nag about when it is going to be done, I grapple my words and say:

"It will be ready when it is dark outside."

Because in all reality, we are ripe when it is dark. When the sun stops shining in our direction and when the torrent blows us through the stormiest of the storms inside, we are ripe.

For forgiveness.

For the empty tomb to reveal our depravity.

For the death that comes before the emerging life.

We make orange Jell-O.

In biological and art history, the color orange symbolizes creativity and intimacy and the portion of the body that releases life (reproductive organs). Beautiful, isn't it? I did not pick orange Jell-O on purpose; it was what was in the cupboard. Sometimes when we are in life's trenches, we have to work with what we already have. Creativity and intimacy are free and forever healing. They cannot be bought in the store, but they can be found in God and within us.

This is often the case when we step into motherhood. We cannot buy all the right answers in the store, but we can look within our journey and find the answers we need. When transforming from a person without children to a mother, we find all sorts of emotions that we want to release. There are extremes everywhere—from the high of ecstatic joy to the grief of a lost identity. There is life, and there is death. There was free time, and now there is none. There was quiet, and now there is crying. There was one child, and now there are sibling squabbles. It is a continual state of grieving an old season and moving into a new one. And yet, as we die to the old way of life, we understand His sacrifice. And when we submit to self-control, to pruning and to sometimes feeling on fire, we become refined and beautified in the process. When we make orange Jell-O, we get to enjoy the treat.

It is a journey. We lose ourselves in self-sacrifice and tame our tongue when we sometimes want to scream. It is a journey: responding to the heights of joy and the simplicities of colored gelatin. We grieve an old way of freedom, and we birth a new way of living. And in the middle, we start to understand who God is.

Day 11

If anyone is in Christ, that person is part of the new creation.
The old things have gone away, and look, new things have arrived!
2 Corinthians 5:17

Motherhood is a combination of grief and life. We step out of one way of living, and we step into a whole new direction. And all of this can occur in the matter of a single day. Everything changes when a child is born, and often the mother is trying to transition into her new role with a lack of sleep, a new understanding of how the world works, and much grief in which to reconcile. *Grief* is a general term used simply to express the idea of letting the old pass away; it is a perfectly normal emotion and experience when transitioning. What often happens in the swirl of new life is that the mother forgets there is also an opportunity to both honor and grieve the old way of doing things. When we are honest with ourselves and can honor the process of passing from the old to the new, we can experience more abundance in the present and in the future. As a mom struggles with the guilt of missing her old life, it actually is not anything to feel bad about. Instead, it is an opportunity to be honest with yourself that the transitional feelings from an old lifestyle to a new lifestyle are healthy.

What are some activities or simple joys that you used to do before having children? How many of those activities can you still incorporate somehow, even just a little bit, into your life now? What emotions do you have as a new parent that make you struggle? Feel guilty? Not want to face? Those emotions are usually just signals of areas in your life that you want to express and honor. After they are expressed in a healthy way (write, run, create, dance, etc.), then they can be released.

A Simple Prayer

Jesus, help me to allow the process of grief to flow from me.
Give me the grace to let the old way of life go gracefully,
so that I am free to be present in my new life.

Day 12

Out of his fullness we have all received grace in place of grace already given.
John 1:16 NIV

Whether simply dealing with emotions that arise when you think of the way life used to be or working through the emotions of what is often called "mom guilt," a mom will often come face-to-face with the inner emotional experience taking on the role of motherhood. Sometimes it is easy to get caught up in the concept that we have to be happy with our role as a mom all the time, and that if we struggle or are unsure or have made mistakes, that we have done something majorly wrong. Mom guilt often invades our consciences when we simply just need a break or need an opportunity to be a person again without a role.

Being a mother can sometimes feel like a job with no break, and at many times it is. On the days when you feel that the wheels are burning dimly and you are tempted to feel badly about your parenting skills (or when we try to fix every-single-mistake-we-may-or-may-not-have-made), give yourself a bit of self-care. This is the perfect time not to overanalyze but to relax and enjoy. It is the perfect time to honor yourselves and your humanity, all the hard work you have done, and move forward with new self-confidence.

Motherhood is hard work. Although there are books about it, there is not a manual for each of your particular children. You have been chosen to be their mother, and in the mistakes and in the joys, you are the best woman for the job.

What are some areas of mom guilt that you repeatedly struggle with? What are some mistakes you have made that you would like to bring correction to? What are some mistakes that you just need to let go (perfection is demeaning)? What are some ways in which you are a great mom? Breathe in self-confidence.

A Simple Prayer

Jesus, help me to release the mom guilt. Help me to give myself grace,
to receive new life from You, and to let go of hindrances that bring anxiety instead of
peace.

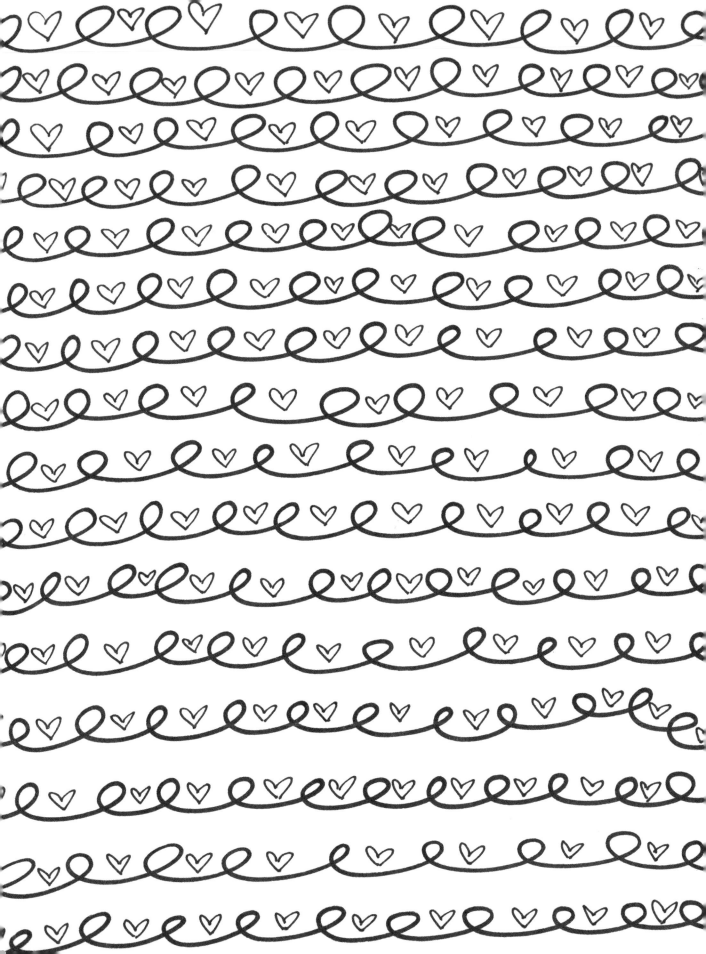

Day 13

Cry out in sorrow, mourn, and weep! Let your laughter become
mourning and your joy become sadness.
James 4:9

Grief can come in many forms during motherhood, often in cases of miscarriage, loss of a child, the quiet of an empty nest, or even walking through infertility. Sometimes we go through these transitions personally, and other times we help carry the burden of a friend who goes through difficulties. When motherhood reflects such a great loss, it can be extremely fragile, hard to understand, and confusing. To celebrate new life and then to grieve in aftermath creates a whirlwind of emotions that need honest attending to. There is no magical formula to make deep loss disappear, but there are steps that can be taken to create an environment for sacred space as the loss is honored and navigated through. It's common to ask why and to have many questions related to loss, sometimes questions that don't seem to be answered on this side of Heaven. Yet, in this season of reflection and healing, there is time to honor areas in our lives or other mothers' lives that may have been stunted before they had a chance to bloom. It's a time of gentleness, to allow the feelings to flow and to await the gift of healing, because even in loss, God can show us His greatness.

What are some simple ways to honor deep loss during motherhood? What are some avenues for releasing pain in a healthy way? If you have experienced loss personally, how can you exhibit self-care in a way that nourishes your soul? If you are walking with a friend who is experiencing loss in motherhood, what are some simple acts of kindness that would help lighten the burden she is experiencing? A good friend can help heal grief with the simplicity of presence and awareness.

A Simple Prayer

Jesus, with each loss of life, may You fill us up. Help us to be honest
in our grief and be available to Your healing.

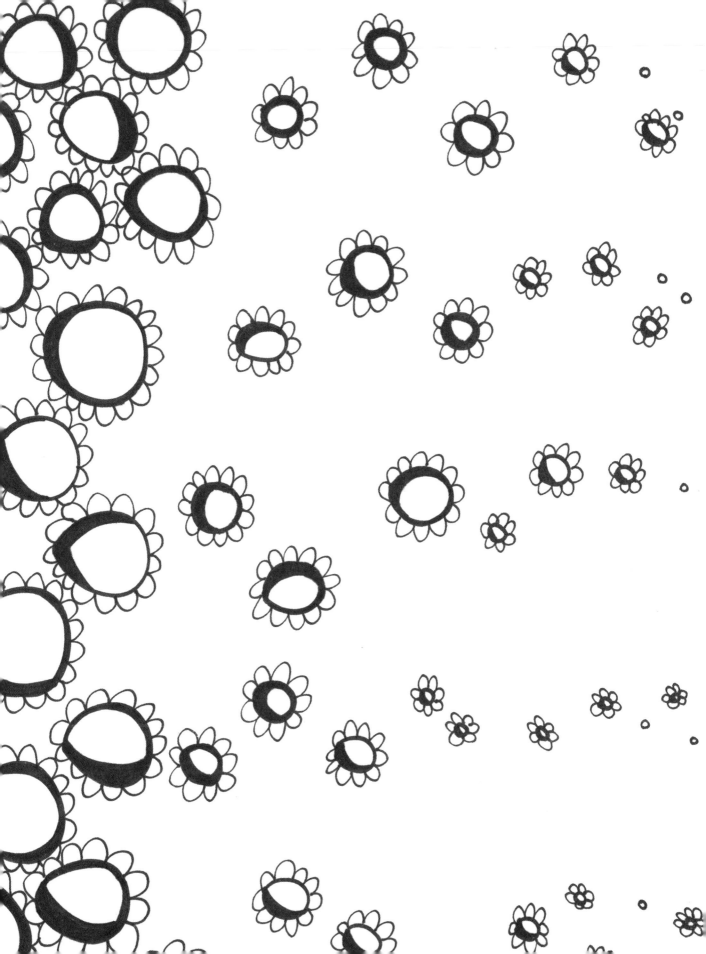

Day 14

Know this: the LORD takes
personal care of the faithful.
The LORD will hear me
when I cry out to him.
Psalm 4:3

In many ways, we grieve emotionally over how our schedules, time, and way of life completely change as we welcome a new child. In addition to this, we also grieve the way our bodies, faces, and general appearance change as we have stretched and grown and released a person into this world. Pregnancy takes its toll on our body, stress often manifests itself in a few more wrinkles than we would like, and we may carry more weight or a muffin top that we did not have before. It is this beautiful process that also causes us to look at ourselves and wonder, "What happened to me?" There is a balance between saying goodbye to a physique we once had and also stewarding the new one we now have. Movement is created in our lives by letting go of old ideals while giving acceptance to the way we look presently; moving into self-care preserves the health and body we have been given. Walking out of the old body and into the new body takes peace, hope, and motion. The best way to care for ourselves is gentleness and forward momentum. So as we say goodbye to a flat stomach and hello to a few stretch marks, we accept the price we paid for carrying life. And then we move forward to steward this new body and appearance. We honor what we have been given. And if it is a bit of work, then the challenge is always healthy.

What are a few simple ways you can heal after childbirth? A little face cream and a walk can go a long way. How can you bring back some self-confidence after your body has transformed and is still coming back to a healed and whole state? Choosing a good diet is key to healing well. Healthy food and vitamins bring healing and helpful transformation. How can you add a few more fruits and vegetables to your regimen?

A Simple Prayer

Jesus, thank You for this transformation in life.
Help me to honor my health and well-being in the midst of such a
great transition in my schedule, my time, and my body.

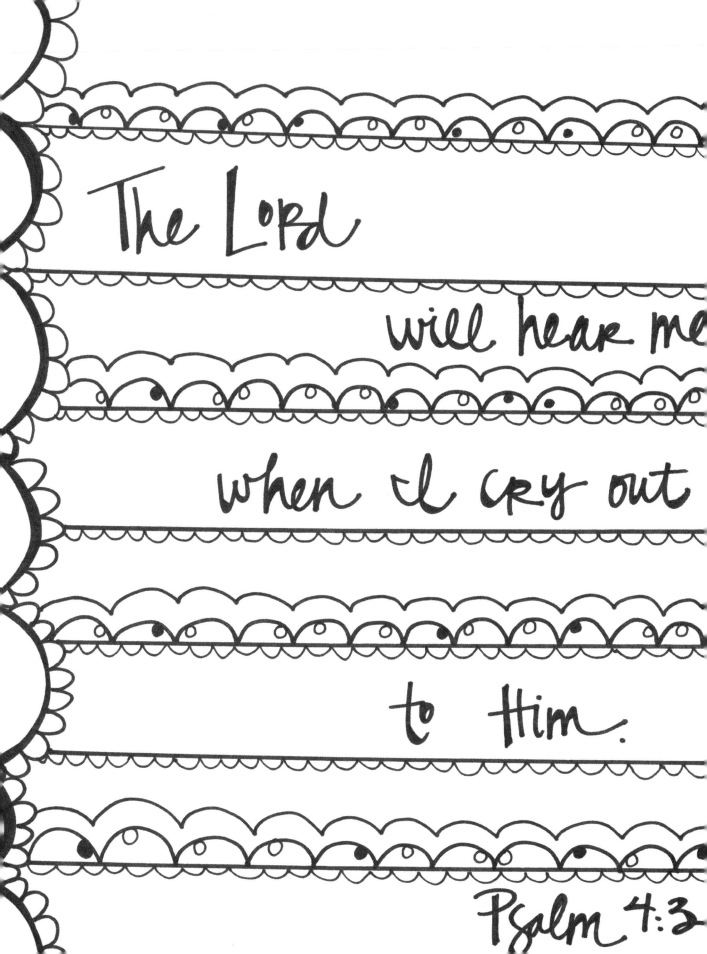

The Lord will hear me when I cry out to Him.

Psalm 4:3

Day 15

Therefore my heart is glad, and my glory rejoices; My flesh also will rest in hope.
Psalm 16:9 NKJV

Acceptance is the key to happiness. When grief comes our way and when new life comes our way, we learn how to process. We say good-bye to what once was, and we say hello to what we now get to receive. In the midst of it, we accept. We honor, we grow, and we accept our current stature with gentleness. It is in this place of self-acceptance that we can see God move in our midst. And when we acknowledge what God is doing, we can face each day with a grateful and peaceful heart. We can live our day with joy and compassion. We can nurture our children with the same love we have been nurtured with by our Heavenly Father. In the transition, we start to see parts of ourselves that we did not know before. We start to experience love in a way that moves toward unconditional measures, and we start to live the way we were created to. Motherhood is a wonderful process full of highs and lows, and we get to experience it all! We have created new life, and now we continue to move forward with courage, vulnerability, and truth.

How can you celebrate today? How can you celebrate where you are and what you have become? Look back on God's faithfulness and practice gratitude. Accept yourself for the brave woman that you are; be open to the surprises God has in store for you!

A Simple Prayer

Jesus, please show me what true acceptance looks like in my life.
Help me live a life in faith and vulnerability and with
great care and excitement for the future.

Unworthiness and the Comparison Game

One of the best ways to thwart unworthiness or comparison is to look for the good.

If we struggle with feeling unworthy or comparing ourselves to other moms, it does not mean that we are a mess. It means that we need a personal upgrade. It just means that at some point, we lost the joy of who we are and we need to reconnect with ourselves.

Several years ago, I started on a proactive journey to find out who God made me to be. God provided clues in advance for me to see that I would face many challenges. In reality, it was really kind of Him to be so reaffirming when I faced a desert. *He is always handing me treasure maps!*

It is not as if identity is a new topic in our society. It can feel as if everyone is trying to find herself these days. I have had the opportunity to "be myself" many times in my life—but with this season of life called motherhood, it felt more definitive. There was an actual and physical shift in my life that made this identity come into a much clearer picture. This shift has four names: Ella, Micah (who is now with Jesus), Lucy, and Oliver.

Becoming a mother is a new season of identity. It brings forth parts of us that are beautiful and nurturing and natural, and it also opens up broken parts in need of beauty, of nurturing, and of natural love.

When God hands us a miracle, sometimes it feels like we have to learn how to help it live and grow and survive and thrive. And this can turn into a confidence builder and a self-esteem crusher all at the same time.

Typically, when our self-esteem has taken a beating with bad toddler behavior or sleepless nights or other unplanned circumstances, it is easy to want to look at ourselves in a dim light and then compare ourselves to the mom next door who always seems to have it together.

Here is the funny part though: no mother has it all together. We are all trying to figure this thing out.

So when we brashly want to rear our insecurity or our judgments or our pain, instead let's extend a hand. Let's open the vulnerable door to our hearts to let the light in. Let's remember who God made us to be. Let's remind ourselves and each other that we are exactly what our children need, and they are exactly what we need. Because that is the beauty of how God works; He is always providing for us.

Day 16

*Let us not grow weary while doing good, for in due season
we shall reap if we do not lose heart.*
Galatians 6:9 NKJV

One of the quickest ways to lose your joy in motherhood is unbelief in your worth and mothering abilities. God made you perfectly able and fit for your child's innate needs. What often hinders us from mothering well is unreconciled grief and harboring mistakes and anxiety. Yet even in our areas of weakness, as we submit those to God, they become our biggest assets as parents. Sometimes it is easy to look at other mothers and compare everything from the organic dish soap down to the type of binkie (if you even used a binkie). One thing is for sure: moms need time to be reminded of the divine way in which we became mothers. It was God's hand in our lives. The love of two particular people made a baby that is completely unique and attuned to respond to the gifts and parenting of those two people. It is beautiful, miraculous, and cannot be compared to another family's experience. We can gain wisdom and understanding from other families; we can exchange tips and advice. But when we step onto the slippery slope of thinking that we are not enough or that we are not doing it right or we have failed, we know it is time to step back and realign ourselves. It is great idea to find support in a few close friends during this time—people who can support you in your unique parenting style and who can remind you that you are doing a great job, especially with the hardest and most meaningful job there is!

Are there areas of your identity and/or parenting that tempt you to struggle with comparison? Write these struggles out; the first way to rewire a situation is to acknowledge it. Of what areas of your parenting are you very sure? These are areas where you can share and give. Giving from your successes helps alleviate unworthiness.

A Simple Prayer

*Jesus, please give me the grace to be honest about my successes and my failures as a
mother. Give me opportunities to share my strengths, and give me support to nurture
areas that need growth.*

Day 17

Therefore let us not judge one another anymore, but rather resolve this, not to put a stumbling block or a cause to fall in our brother's way.
Romans 14:13 NKJV

Comparison robs us of joy, contentment, and confidence. Constantly looking at other mothers and the way they parent can turn into our quickest downfall. If you are having a difficult time looking around without judging yourself, then the best thing to do is evaluate. Taking a break from social media or friendships where conversation is not fruitful is a great first step. If you are consistently finding yourself struggling in a certain area, you can find another mother who has walked your path. Often times, we can find support and strength in friendships with women who have struggled in similar areas of identity and mothering. When they have overcome, their advice can give you some tools for your journey to do the same.

When struggling with comparison, it is best to set boundaries with what triggers you and find support with those who can build into you. It is the best of both worlds, and you can gain forward momentum both with your weaknesses and with your strengths.

What are areas in your mothering where you often fall into comparison? What are skills you would like to grow? What are weaknesses you would like to strengthen? Who can help support you in your journey? Find an accountability friendship, someone who will challenge you to be you and also give you the support needed to make that a reality.

A Simple Prayer

Jesus, thank You for giving me the life I have.
Would You give me access to the support I need for
growth, maturity, and joy as a mother?

Day 18

Wherever there is jealousy and selfish ambition, there is disorder and
everything that is evil.
James 3:16

The first step for practicing self-awareness is opening our eyes and ears to limiting beliefs about ourselves. When we recognize where our triggers are (jealousy, comparison, negative self-talk), it gives us the opportunity to find a solution. Many times the negative feeling we are experiencing is actually just the shadow and opposite of who we are meant to be. If we are jealous, we really need connection to our true selves. If we compare ourselves to others, we really are just looking for validation of our identity. If we talk or think negatively about ourselves, it is an opportunity to find a friend who can remind us of our true worth. Small steps lead to big changes. When trying to connect with your true self, fuel your energy toward what is good. If you are a working mom who would like to stay at home, look into a few ways that you can make money from home. If you are a stay-at-home mom and feel the need to work outside the home, look for a way to do that but still maintain your time with your children. If you wish your child would behave better, look inside yourself at what behavior you can change. Kids mimic their parents. If you wish your child would listen to you, listen to them. If you wish you had more mother friends, go to the park and be a friend. If you wish your mom body was back to prepregnancy weight, take your kids for a walk. You will thank yourself in a million ways. Comparison breeds bitterness, and movement breeds joy!

What is a small step forward that you can make today for growth? What is a limiting belief that you struggle with? Write the *opposite* of the limiting belief on a note card and place it on the bathroom mirror. Remind yourself often: "This is who *I am*."

A Simple Prayer

Jesus, give me the grace and the bravery to be self-aware.
Help me see the joy in my identity so that I can be whole
and also a better steward of my environment.

Day 19

*I'm also asking you, loyal friend, to help these women who have struggled
together with me in the ministry of the gospel, along with Clement
and the rest of my coworkers whose names are in the scroll of life.*
Philippians 4:3

One of the best ways to build a good support system is to leave behind unhealthy relationships. Motherhood is a vulnerable and emotional time, and it is important to be particular about whom you let into your life during this season. If someone is repeatedly setting you up for failure with limiting beliefs, the first step is to take constructive criticism into account, and the second step is to make a healthy boundary for yourself. It does not mean all relationships have to go to the curb, but it does mean that reevaluating your support system at this time may be important. Self-esteem and joy are vital to mothering well. If you are supported well, you can be the best mother you want to be. If the support you have been leaning on is not grounded in goodness, it is an appropriate time to look at other avenues for nurturing your soul. A happy mother is a confident mother, and you deserve to be the best!

Think about some areas in your life that could be hindering your innate support system. It could be people, unhealthy food, time wasted in unfruitful ways, or many other things. Remind yourself that you deserve the best. Remember to allow for constructive criticism but also surround yourself with people and support that are trying to build you up. You have every right to be particular! Your motherhood depends on it.

A Simple Prayer

*Jesus, thank You for being my ultimate support system. Please give me wisdom in
choosing the friends and relationships that I bring close to me during this season.
Help me to receive constructive criticism; help me to understand my innate worth.*

dream. believe. fly.

Day 20

God also vouched for their message with signs, amazing things, various miracles, and gifts from the Holy Spirit, which were handed out the way he wanted.
Hebrews 2:4

Nurturing confidence and identity (outside of mothering) is a great tool for self-growth and gaining new skills. One of the best ways to be a great mother is actually to forget you are mother every once in a while! Sharpening personal skills and gifting, outside of mothering, brings you back to a clearer version of yourself and a clearer version of your kids. Mothering is new and challenging. Remembering old gifts and talents you had before becoming a mother helps you stay balanced and keeps you out of your own head. Identity is key to great mothering. A mom who is happy with herself and the growing version of herself is happy when nurturing the growing versions of those around her, even in the midst of temper tantrums, dirty diapers, and sleepless nights.

Be kind to yourself! Remember the joys of your own childhood and identity. Do not let the responsibilities of your new life steal the joy you had when all you had to manage was yourself. Go on a creative date all by yourself. Choose a day on the calendar, mark it down, and go do something you used to do all the time. Remember the ease of freedom and a carefree existence!

A Simple Prayer

Jesus, thank You for who You have created me to be before becoming a mother. Help me to remember who I was when responsibility was not at the forefront; help me to remember how to play.

Self-Acceptance and Peace

I love that word. *Acceptance.*

Acceptance has been my magic ticket to peace. Kind of like my youngest, Oliver.

I knew while I was pregnant with my middle, Lucy, that there would also be one more child. And when God surprised us with a plus sign on a pregnancy test, I was not surprised—because I knew I needed him. His little life would help me find this peace and acceptance I had been looking for.

There is something about having a third child and going to zone-defense as a daily routine that teaches me peace. The house will not be perfect. My energy will be spread more thinly across the board. I do not have enough hands for each child. If more than one person is talking, I cannot possibly answer them all. It is chaos. But it is beautiful chaos.

The days I find myself most stressed out about my house being totally out of control are the days I am not willing to accept that I am living in a season where my house is just going to be totally out of control. It does not mean that I am lazy and do not take steps to clean out the oven after I have neglected it for the last five years (wait, what?). No, it just means that I focus on the task at hand, and I *let the rest of it go.*

I have been the queen of nervous exhaustion. Add to that three kids that are three years old and under, and you get a hot mess. A hot mess, I tell ya. And the worst part about it all? The fact that I just would not accept it. Well, until about now. (OK, really, I am still working on it.)

But that is the ticket: learning to accept where we are. If we never get to the acceptance part, we will always be trying to fix something. And if I am always trying to fix something, then I am not enjoying anything. I have been given a life to enjoy and three of the cutest little people on the planet to enjoy every single day of it with.

It is part of the reason I love to take pictures of my kids so often; it fills me with gratitude. I see from a new perspective. And when I see from a new perspective, I can relish, and in the relishing, I actually move forward. I become more productive (and fuller of love)!

It is amazing and simple, really: accepting that life is somewhat chaotic instead of constantly trying to paddle upstream. We often choose to paddle upstream, that's the crazy part. When we do, we usually have a white-knuckle grip and end up nowhere. At least I do.

And so, I am loosening up. Writing it out. It is so much more wonderful to show up to our own lives—our messy, chaotic, finding-peace-in-the-crazy lives. Because when we do, we actually get to start to dream and build and bloom right in the midst of the dirt and soil and sunshine.

> So let the wheat grow with the tares
> That His glory would be manifest in me
> This has never been about my performance
> But about His Goodness
> So I offer up my Death of self—
> Not because I am unworthy, or not enough, or nothing—that is religion—
> But because when I see the emptiness of manmade effort,
> I absorb the worth of God-made Design
> He never made me nothing
> He always made me something
> And as the wheat grows with the tares
> I see His beauty over me, in me, through me
> So let the Wheat grow with the tares . . .

Day 21

I will praise You, for I am fearfully and wonderfully made;
Marvelous are Your works,
And that my soul knows very well.
Psalm 139:14 NKJV

It is said that a person needs to hear something new almost thirty times before he or she actually starts to believe it. We are on Day 21 of our journey to a joyful motherhood, and if you are not clear what we need most as mothers, here it is again: self-acceptance! The best mothers are the mothers who are well-loved and well-nurtured as women. We already have the perfect and complete acceptance from a loving God; Jesus has made this path straight for us. The next and very crucial step is to love ourselves and care for ourselves. God can love us and care for us, but if we do not love and care for ourselves, we set ourselves up for loss. Of course, support from a loving spouse, our children, and our friends brings abundance to our lives! But we, as women, need to often encourage ourselves to come into a place of self-acceptance and self-love.

List five things about yourself that you absolutely love. List five ways you love your family as well. You are doing a great job!

A Simple Prayer

Jesus, let me see the good in myself. Help me to celebrate who
I am in all the messiness and chaos and beauty that is called new life.

I will praise You; for I am fearfully and wonderfully made. Psalm 139:14

Day 22

But I will remember the Lord's deeds;
yes, I will remember your wondrous acts from times long past.
Psalm 77:11

The problem of self-acceptance can often be traced to the challenges from our childhood. What we often see in ourselves as weak parenting skills are actually patterns that have been passed on to us from the way we were raised. As we see the weak spots, it is important to bring nurture to the lacking areas. When wounds are triggered, it is the perfect opportunity for God to bring healing. After the healing comes, so does the new mindset. We accept God's gift in our lives and then we choose a new behavior. If we are constantly anxious and react toward our children with haste and a loud voice, we need peace in our lives. We need our own trauma healed. We can do this by giving our wounds to God, allowing Him to fill us with His peace, and then choosing a better position of giving. There sometimes are different patterns that have gotten passed down to us that we would like to interrupt and re-create differently for our children. As we accept where we have been and what we need, we can break cycles that do not foster a healthy environment for our family.

What are some patterns in your life or in your parenting that you would like to interrupt? Do you remember where these patterns started? Can you go back to areas in your childhood that might be in need of restoration, give them over to God, and ask Him for new provision in those areas?

A Simple Prayer

Jesus, thank You for the foundation I was given in childhood.
Help me to acknowledge patterns that need to be interrupted and
re-created with honesty, humility, and forgiveness.

Day 23

They will burst into bloom,
and rejoice with joy and singing.
They will receive the glory of Lebanon,
the splendor of Carmel and Sharon.
They will see the Lord's glory,
the splendor of our God.
Isaiah 35:2

Bloom where you are planted; it is the best way to start loving and accepting yourself. When we learn how to build where we are, we take baby steps toward significance. There are small choices we can make daily that can help propel us into a life and motherhood full of joy, peace, and abundance. Once we start becoming seasoned in our own healing work, we start to live with much more fervor and gratitude. It is often the small, daily choices we make that bring us to a place of inner peace and gratitude. In the slow and steady of life, we make progress. If self-acceptance were a skin-care regimen, we would see great results with daily use over a period of time. A facial is wonderful every once in a while to go deeper and to enhance what we are already doing, but the overall most sustainable changes come from our daily disciplines. This is how we bloom where we are.

What can we do now for self-acceptance? Do you need to be heard? Write in a journal or tell a story. Do you need understanding? Find a friend who is a great listener. Do you need support? Ask for help. It almost seems obvious, but self-acceptance often lies in the simple. From the small choice to step toward your true nature, you start to shift the stress and self-rejection out of your heart.

How can you bloom where you are planted? Are there any friendships, groups, clubs that you can invest in where you will also be able to grow in self-confidence? What is a small but steady goal in one area of your life that you would like to pursue? Diet, exercise, faith, skin care, parenting skills, a hobby (writing, dancing, cooking)? Give yourself permission to start in baby steps toward a dream or goal that has always been in your heart.

A Simple Prayer

Jesus, give me the vision to start with small steps of self-acceptance in the here and now.
Help me to be diligent in my daily disciplines so that I can become the best version of myself.

Bloom

from the inside out.

Day 24

You've given me the shield of your salvation;
your strong hand has supported me;
your help has made me great.
Psalm 18:35

Once you start growing in your own self-confidence and gifts, find a group where you can get connected. Whether it is a small group of friends, a church, a class, or a club, finding a place to invest in is key to growing and blooming well. With the support and encouragement of other people, you will see the fruit of your life grow exponentially. Surround yourself with people who want to see you do well as a person and as a parent. Surround yourself with people who have resources and wisdom to share with you and who you can also support with your own wisdom and resources. As the exchange grows between your true self-acceptance, personal growth, and the opportunities presented by a support system, you will see your spirit being filled up in new and exciting ways. You will also see this happen for your children because they love a mom who is happy. As you bloom, so will they.

After you have found a place to plug in, ask God how He might want you to participate. Sometimes we just need friendship and rest without much activity (because moms are always active); other times we are ready to serve in a more formal context through a part-time job or as a leader within an organization (a coach, or teacher, and so on). Be aware of what is best for your particular situation! You know your limits, and you also know your goals. Choose what is right for you and start to build into your new future!

A Simple Prayer

Thank You, Jesus, for my gifts and desires. Help me to plug into the right community, with the right time requirements, and where my goals and dreams are supported.

Your help. has made me. great.

Psalm 18:35

Day 25

Strength and honor are her clothing;
she is confident about the future.
Proverbs 31:25

Dare to dream! When basic needs are met and our self-concept is healthy and alive, there is plenty of room to play. This is where, as mothers, we give ourselves the opportunity to explore and create. We give ourselves room to hope and wish and dream, continually bringing us into a place of discovery, growth, newfound freedom, self-care, and generosity for others. Every mother has her own unique desires for her family and calling. Some moms want to homeschool, to bring their kids in closely, and to dream as a unit in this way. Other moms may send their children to school while they continue to prepare their home or take care of other children. Other mothers may want to reenter the workforce and have their family get involved in community-centered service projects. Still other families may get really connected within a church body. There are so many options, and not one way is designated as the right way. There are many right ways! It is at this place that you can choose how you would like to give. Whether it is continuing to build into your own family first (perhaps having more children or just cultivating a healthy and close environment), or extending out to the community in some way, this is the place where dreams become reality. When the mom is healthy and happy, the whole family comes into alignment and into new opportunities to dream and succeed.

What are some of the dreams you have for your family, both short and long term? I always want my family to eat at the dinner table each night (short term), and I also want my family to participate in charity projects together (possibly long term). Work on a short family mission statement which covers your family's values and goals. Who are you as a family and where are you going? Have fun!

A Simple Prayer

Jesus, I want to dream! Align my heart and desires to Your
will so I can dream, explore, and serve my family.

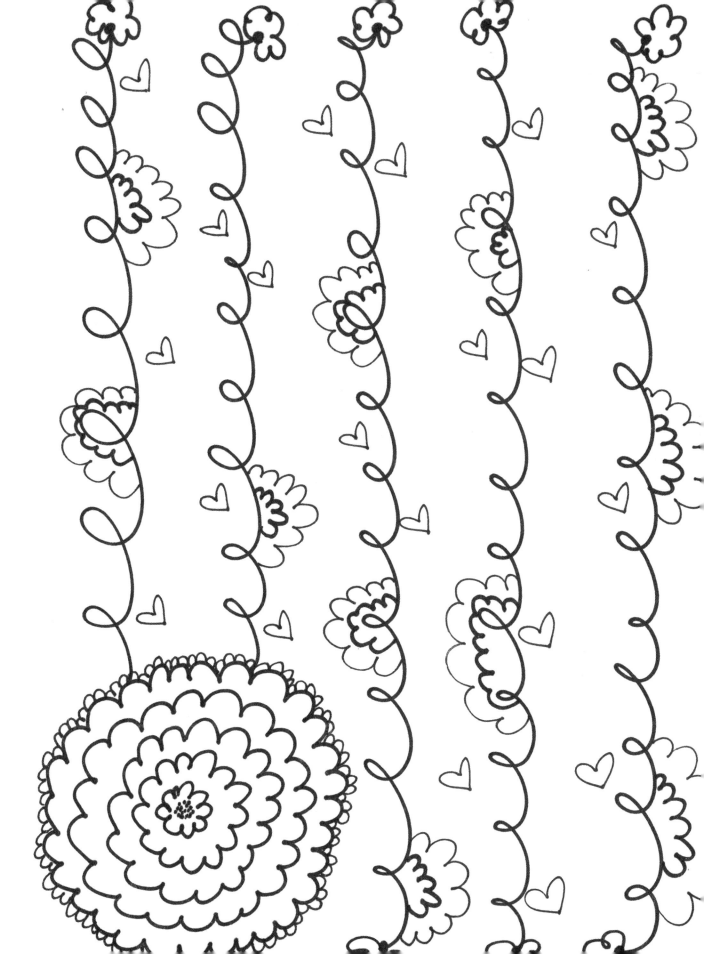

The Cycles of Giving and Self-Care

When David and I bought our first house, we thought it needed something. You know, something that would bring flair and fun and comfort.

So we bought ourselves a Saint Bernard.

Oh, Howie. How I adored him. I couldn't imagine life without him.

He was big and fluffy (sadly, he is now in doggie heaven)—the best pillow around. Every morning, as I would rest my head on his belly, he would rest his giant of a head across my face, and though I could barely breathe, I loved it.

And then I would walk downstairs. I would see dog food all over the kitchen floor. I would sit down on the couch with my cup of hot coffee only to realize I had rested my arm in a two-inch long slobbery goo. And let's not talk about how many times my vacuum cleaner was broken by overuse picking up dog hairs.

But there was something about that gentle giant that wooed me in. Just like love.

Sometimes it is messy, like muddy paws all over the couch. Sometimes it is heavy, like a Saint Bernard who thinks he is a lap dog. Sometimes it is protective, like barking through the window while Ella took her nap. And sometimes it is astonishing, like finding a monster of a dog in our bed eating a bone from the butcher (with blood and meat everywhere). And, of course, I was the one who had to take our oh-so-expensive down comforter to the dry cleaners, trying to convince them that I did not murder anyone.

When it comes down to it, Howie made me a better person. Just like my children do. Just like love does.

Love is patient, love is kind, it isn't jealous,
it doesn't brag, it isn't arrogant, it isn't rude,
it doesn't seek its own advantage, it isn't irritable,
it doesn't keep a record of complaints, it isn't happy with
injustice, but it is happy with the truth. Love puts up
with all things, trusts in all things, hopes for all things,
endures all things.
Love never fails.
1 Corinthians 13:4-8a

Howie comforted parts in me that were broken and in need of a hug. Dogs have amazing healing power. He cuddled at just the right time. He sat at attention waiting for his treat like the sweetest of army soldiers. He made me laugh as he scavenged under Ella's high chair eagerly awaiting a dropped blueberry. And the games he would play! He scratched at the door for an hour to come inside, and every time I got to the door to open it, he ran away (and smiled). He liked to play, and sometimes it tested my patience. It highlighted the parts in me that still needed a little lovin': just like the muddy paws and the slobber on the walls and the chunk of our budget labeled "lint rollers."

But it is a beautiful paradox, isn't it? Kind of like marriage. Kind of like parenting. A lot like Love.

If dogs are symbolic of compassion, then every mom should have one. There is something in the love of a dog that covers and nourishes us in the messiness, in the exercise, and in the picking up huge bags of dog food at the grocery store. So much of having a Saint Bernard taught me about the healing power of generosity and of sharing love. And just as much, it taught me about how to care and nurture myself and let myself just be.

Kids are the same way. They teach us how to love and how to give. They also teach us where the end of our rope is so that we learn how to take care of ourselves. We learn how to place limits on our giving so we can fill up with our own healing.

Giving is what mothers do. It just is. And if the love of a mother could be bottled into a pet, it would be as big as a Saint Bernard.

Day 26

But this I say: He who sows sparingly will also reap sparingly, and he
who sows bountifully will also reap bountifully. So let each one give as he
purposes
in his heart, not grudgingly or of necessity; for God loves a cheerful giver.
2 Corinthians 9:6-7 NKJV

The default mode of a mother is giver. Giver of life, giver of time, giver of nurture. If there is any type of serving required, a mother learns how to do it. As moms, we give all day long, often to those who cannot help themselves (especially in the early years). Caretaking is a genuine gift but can also be taxing without the proper boundaries. Self-care is the key to giving well and with purity. Managing these boundaries, self-care, and generosity looks like a dance; it takes practice, rhythm, and learning how to flow to the music. Because as we are cared for by the Greatest Giver of all, we learn how to start releasing that same care into the people around us.

The first step is always to listen. Take a few minutes of quiet time to ask God what it is that you need from God today. How can you understand God's nature as a Giver today? When we see our lack, we can receive His fullness. Becoming self-aware to the basic needs you have can bring about the joy you receive in order to fill in the basic needs of your family.

A Simple Prayer

Jesus, thank You for being the Greatest Giver of Life. Give me the grace to walk in your flow of generosity, tending to my own self-care and then overflowing to others around me.

Day 27

*Finally, brethren, whatever things are true, whatever things are noble,
whatever things are just, whatever things are pure, whatever things are
lovely, whatever things are of good report, if there is any virtue and if there is
anything praiseworthy—meditate on these things.*
Philippians 4:8 NKJV

It is important for you to know, as a person and as a mother, what fills you up. How do you fuel your love tank? Some call these Love Languages (how we give and receive love), and they are definitely that. Do you like quality time? quiet time? a hug? a walk? being served? serving? The list can go on and on. The key to filling up your life with thanksgiving is to find the ways in which you can replace the love and life you give away on a regular basis. As we communicate to others around us the ways in which we receive love, we can also learn the best ways in which they give and receive love. And when we are in the stream, stemming from the perfect love of God, we are able to ebb and flow with the nature of generosity. Our family becomes like a river, no one lacking but always moving forward and producing life where it is needed.

Spend some time honing in on your favorite ways to be loved. Share those with your family. Think of ways that you can incorporate this kind of love into your life daily so that you always feel like you have been refreshed in a way that helps you serve better.

A Simple Prayer

*Jesus, help me to remember myself in the giving. Remind me of the ways I feel most
nurtured.*
*Help me to remember to nourish myself daily as a devotion and honor to You and to
myself.*

Day 28

Love suffers long and is kind; love does not envy; love does not parade itself,
is not puffed up; does not behave rudely, does not seek its own, is not provoked,
thinks no evil; does not rejoice in iniquity, but rejoices in the truth;
bears all things, believes all things, hopes all things, endures all things.
1 Corinthians 13:4-7 NKJV

After we learn how we like to receive love, it is equally important to figure out our favorite way to give love. Sometimes they are the same, and sometimes they are different. When we can highlight the ways in which we like to give, it opens us to more outlets through which to fill up our love tank as mothers. Motherhood is almost one constant motion, and it is important to know where we can get small charges of energy here and there. Finding ways to serve that provide us with joy keeps us fresh and alive; it serves our hearts and souls while also being able to provide tangibly. Soon enough, these favorite ways of receiving love and sharing love can give us the capacity to give out in ways that may not be as natural for us but that might be most important to those around us.

Think about your favorite ways to share love. What are a few tangible tasks that you love performing for your family? (It is important to write them down and remember them for future use when you might feel low on love.) In the giving, we can always receive; sometimes we just need to find the right outlet.

A Simple Prayer

Jesus, help me to recognize my favorite ways to give love.
Show me opportunities to love well in ways that I enjoy.

Day 29

I give you a new commandment: Love each other.
Just as I have loved you, so you also must love each other.
John 13:34

After we take responsibility for ourselves and the ways in which we enjoy receiving and giving love, we have a great capacity within us to nurture the ways our loved ones give and receive love. Sometimes the way our family accepts love is contrary to our inherent nature, but since we have learned how to cultivate our own "love life," we now have the capacity to give from a full well. Take time to listen and to ask your family how they best receive and give love. Because of the God-given functions of a family, we often find that where we have deficits, our family has filling. And where our family has deficits, we have filling. Sometimes what we most need is just to be aware of those needs and full of knowledge. Set aside time today to ask your family about their favorite ways to learn, love, and grow. Write them down and keep them in a place where you can continue to revert back to them. Make a small goal this week to both give in a way your family receives and also to give in a way you love. Watch the responses that follow.

How did you feel this week? Did you have more energy? What worked well? What might need tweaking?

A Simple Prayer

Jesus, thank You for filling up my well! Give me listening ears
to honor the way my family members receive love.

Day 30

*May the Lord cause you to increase and enrich your love for
each other and for everyone in the same way as we also love you.*
1 Thessalonians 3:12

Sometimes the best way to give and receive love in your family is intimate connection and one-on-one dates. Quality time with those you love in a setting that is focused and without distractions makes for the best kind of exchange. If you are married, it is equally important to have time with your husband as it is with your kids because out of your marriage will flow the teamwork that your children need to thrive. One-on-one dates with your kids (especially if there are multiple children) will also give them a time for safe expression, making choices, and the intimate connection that may have started to give way to the tasks of the day and managing a household. Connection is the key to giving well. Without connection, the generosity will feel stagnant and like a chore instead of an outflow of healthy love.

Choose days on the calendar each month as date nights for yourself as well as your family. Make time in your busy schedule for your entire family but also one-on-one intimate time. Let your children choose what they would like to do. Give them a chance to express the connection they need and would like with you. As you do this, you will find that your giving will grow, and it will be more fulfilling for your time together.

A Simple Prayer

*Jesus, help us to carve out sacred time for connection as a family.
Give us opportunities for one-on-one depth and intimacy.*

May the Lord
cause you to
increase
and
enrich
your
love
for
each
other.

1 Thessalonians 3:12

Placing an Emphasis on Presence

There are many, many reasons why I am grateful for my kids. Their smiles, their wit, their vivacious love of life—even if it just means going to the grocery store or to the bank. And then there is the gratitude I ensue from the hard lessons they teach me. You know, all that stuff about myself I did not want to look at until I am faced with it in front of little eyes? Yes, those lessons. I am grateful for my children showing me the hard things, not even intentionally, but just in the way they react to life. Yet, out of all the joys and the difficult days, I think what I most appreciate about my kids is that they teach me how to be present—and that teaches me how to be loved. All kids really want is for their parents to be *with* them. Most of the time it does not even matter what we are doing, just as long as we are together. And it is in those small moments of being together that I can appreciate the idiosyncrasies of each of them. It is when we slow down that I notice that there is a dimple under Ella's right eye that shows itself when she smiles (or cries). It is when we slow down that Lucy comes crawling over to me just to hug my neck. It is when we slow down that sibling rivalry also weakens and takes a breath.

It is in the slowdown.

There is peace. And there is presence.

It seems that in a world of "doing," everything tries to steal away from this time of presence. Make sure the house is spotless. Make sure you are at this activity or that function. Make sure the clothes are washed and ironed. Make sure dinner is cooked (and always organic). Make sure they get time to exercise. Make sure *you* get time to exercise. Make sure you do not lose contact with the outside world. Make sure you are following the guidelines in this parenting how-to book. Make sure . . . Make sure . . . Make sure.

All of a sudden I am tired.

But when I am present, I am not so tired. It does not mean that I still do not fall hard into my pillow each night—because I surely do. It is tiring with a baby on your hip, a baby in your belly, and a three-year-old holding onto your hand. And yet, the load is lifted for all of us when we are present.

When I am not looking over what I "should be doing for them," I am enjoying them. When I am not thinking of the list of other to do's that so easily stack up, it is easy to respond favorably to: "Mama do it" and "Can we play outside?" and "Let's go to the store!"

I have a pastor friend who once shared how a newborn baby can be compared to the Presence of God. It is one of my favorite metaphors. When that baby shows up, everything is focused on it. Feed the baby, change the baby, and hold the baby when he or she is crying. We steward everything around the new life we have been given. And even though we have multiple babies and responsibilities that have to be shared, it is still the same.

So many of the problems in our world revolve around the fact that our families are broken—that we cannot steward what we have (and then usually just stack more activity on top of it). The statistics of fatherless kids are horrific. Families fight; people do not talk to one another.

If we lived in a world that slowed down, that was not quite so productive, that was not so ill-equipped with false responsibility, I think we might find more peace. I think if we lived with a messier house during the day, we might make room for more creativity instead of just clean kitchen floors.

I find this peace in the presence of my family. They are presents to me. They teach me presence. And in presence, love is found. And so are acceptance and joy and laughter.

It is definitely a treat when a mom gets an opportunity to get to the outside world for self-care. I might get a pedicure or an afternoon to myself, but I find that I can start to get bored after a few hours away. I long for the presence again.

And that is the real gift of motherhood.

Day 31

*The L*ORD *is my shepherd.*
I lack nothing.
He lets me rest in grassy meadows;
he leads me to restful waters.
Psalm 23:1-2

What a mother most often yearns for is a heart of rest. When we are at peace, we are not in need, not in panic, and not in a state of anxiety or depression. In the quiet, we can drink Living Water. Sometimes a vacation from normal life is necessarily to be refreshed and recharged, but more than that, the best type of vacation is when we can be refreshed by our daily lives. When we start to move and live by the hand of our Shepherd, we can be revived and refreshed in even the most energetic and exhausting of circumstances. Let's spend this next five days memorizing Psalm 23. As we quiet ourselves, we can find everything we need within that space.

Memorize verses 1-2 today.

A Simple Prayer

Father, You are my Shepherd. I do not need a thing.
You have given me everything. You have given me rest and
peace during my trials and tribulations. You restore my soul.

Day 32

He keeps me alive.
He guides me in proper paths
for the sake of his good name.
Psalm 23:3

Often times our best way of warfare is to memorize the Bible. Sometimes we just need to remember the Truth. As we go back to the Source, we rewire our minds and our thoughts. When all other plans fail, God does not. Just as He spoke the word and it was, when He speaks over us, we can breathe again. And when we can take a gulp of His original breath in us, we go down the paths of righteousness. We live out lives of peace and joy and good-will toward everyone in our path, especially toward the little ones that He has given us to steward.

Meditate on the goodness of God. Memorize verse 3 today.

A Simple Prayer

True to Your Word Father, You let me catch my breath and send me in
the right direction. Thank You for holding me up when I have fallen
or allowing me to rest in Your arms when I am weak.

Day 33

Even when I walk through the darkest valley,
I fear no danger because you are with me.
Your rod and your staff—
they protect me.
Psalm 23:4

There will always be times of growth and trust in parenting. And even when times get difficult and struggles arise, we remember who loves us. We remember who the biggest supporter of mothers is. When we fail, when we meet challenges that we do not feel prepared for, we can go back to the Source. God loves us. As we give way to children by preparing, birthing, giving, grieving, and resting (and then giving even more), we end up back at the Source. He is the Alpha and the Omega; He is the beginning and the end. Everything we need for life and godliness are found in Him. God is there in the darkest of nights and in the brightest of mornings, and He keeps us safe and secure by reminding us of His love.

Memorize verse 4 today.

A Simple Prayer

Heavenly Father, even when my pathway goes through Death Valley,
I will not be afraid when You walk at my side. Your trusty Shepherd's crook
makes me feel secure. I know that You are there to protect me
from any evil that tries to attack me.

Day 34

You set a table for me
right in front of my enemies.
You bathe my head in oil;
my cup is so full it spills over!
Psalm 23:5

In our Father and in our circumstances, we have everything we need to eat. There is always enough food for us. He leads us into all the right circumstances to feed our souls. No matter what is going on around us, He always has enough resources for us.

As a mother, when comparison and perfectionism can run their course, we need to be reminded that we have everything we need to thrive. We are the best mothers possible for our children. God gave us the DNA we have for a purpose, and it matches the DNA of our children for their purpose. As we are honest with our own emotions, we close the gaps between what we lack within our own lives. As we close those gaps, we automatically set ourselves up to help bridge and nurture any gaps in our children's lives. We become prepared as we nurture what we have been given. As our heart stays open to forgiveness, we become whole. And as we become whole, we make our children whole. It is a beautiful cycle. We forever drink of blessings.

Memorize verse 5 today.

A Simple Prayer

Jesus, You serve me a six-course dinner right in front of my enemies.
You revive my drooping head; my cup brims with blessings.
It is my prayer that any blessings that I receive I give back to those around me.

Day 35

Yes, goodness and faithful love
will pursue me all the days of my life,
and I will live in the LORD's house
as long as I live.
Psalm 23:6

Make a point to remember, each and every day, that motherhood is beautiful. In each diaper change and each cutting of mini-sandwiches, a mother gets to live a life of peace and joy and serenity. A mother gets to nurture her children. This is the beauty of God in your midst. With each death of your old self and your old mindset, there is great life. And as mothers, we are blessed to be the ones who get to steward that gift. Our bodies actually manifest heaven coming to earth; we are the home for creating a human being. No one else has the privilege to do so, and it is an honor. Being a mother is honorable, worthy, and like no other gift this earth contains. Just as Mary birthed Jesus, we have the privilege of birthing great grace. And as we do, we see His beauty and love chase after us in every circumstance, whether it is a challenge or a blessing.

Memorize verse 6 today.

A Simple Prayer

Jesus, Your beauty and love chase after me every day of my life.
I am back home in Your house for the rest of my life.

Your love & beauty chase after me...

Psalm 23:6

Living a Lifestyle of Forgiveness

"I'm living outrageously loved—and that jolly well settles it." A British man named Graham Cooke said that.

I certainly have felt that since having children. It is amazing how the gift of a new baby can do that—make us feel loved—even in the midst of a lack of sleep and exhausted bodies and . . . and . . . and. There is a certain ecstasy with children; they are the evidence of a miracle.

There is a paradox when you consider the definition of *love*. *Unconditional love* means that there are no limits or conditions; it is complete love. There's no settling when it comes to real love. It always sees the good, and as a result, the not so good behavior has a chance to fall by the wayside. It is constantly seeking to encourage, to bring life, and to shut down death. Real love is life.

And we were made for eternal living.

Yes, our human bodies will fail us at some time. But thank God this is not all we have going for us.

Think about this perspective of love and learn the art of forgiveness—which essentially is the art of giving, of generosity, of living outrageously loved.

We had a beautiful time of praying over our little Lucy at a friend's house when she was a baby. One of our guests told us that Lucy would carry a spirit of generosity with her—and that she would always be giving out to others. She said our tendency might be to try to guard her so as not to let her be abused, but that this would not happen. It seems that our Lucy would have the strategic wisdom to give powerfully.

Isn't that beautiful?

Children are such gifts from God. They birth in us who we were created to be from the very beginning. I love that.

Even from her time in my womb and the three years she has had on this earth, her generous spirit teaches me love. She teaches me how to give, to forgive, and to live outrageously loved.

And living loved is why we are here. *It's our purpose.*

I love being loved. Not because I am insecure—though there are surely spots in me that are still in the process of becoming fully secure. I love being loved because that is why God made me. To be cherished.

And He fully blesses that love when I give it away.

This gives life meaning, and it is the absolutely happiest way to grow. No storm can weather our path when we live a life loved. No discipline or correction makes us second guess ourselves because living a life loved is always about being called higher. From glory to glory.

And so, it is this ebb and flow of glory. Receiving love and then giving it out. And each time, my joy bubble increases and increases. Fear disappears. Forgiveness is innate. Life tastes good.

We are saved by grace so that none of us can boast about our blessings. They are a gift from God. We are fully accepted into the generous heart of our Father (see Ephesians 2:8; Isaiah 53:3).

Day 36

And whenever you stand praying, if you have anything against anyone, forgive him, that your Father in heaven may also forgive you your trespasses.
Mark 11:25 NKJV

Out of an inner position of gratitude and abundance, we can give and forgive. Our children are just that, children. We are the ones who teach them how to process, forgive, and respond to circumstances. When our cup is full, we can overflow with wisdom and blessing as an example to them. It is our own inner journey that provides us the means to give to our children well. Though there will always be mistakes as we are human, it is in the process of forgiveness that we can work through old cycles, hurtful words or actions, and failures. Children are some of the most forgiving and resilient people on the planet. Even though everything will not always go as planned, we can always communicate through hard circumstances in order to come up with a better solution. The essence of motherhood is forgiveness: to give in advance. We give our family love because He first loved us.

Brainstorm a few ways that you can give in advance to your family today. What are a few simple gestures that would show them how much you care for them?

A Simple Prayer

Jesus, thank You for Your forgiveness.
Thank You for giving to me in advance.
Help me to receive Your grace and give it to others.

Day 37

Praise the Lord!
Oh, give thanks to the Lord, for He is good!
For His mercy endures forever.
Psalm 106:1 NKJV

Forgiveness is an act of giving, listening, nurturing, setting boundaries, and letting go. It is a pattern that creates both roots and wings. When we are the ones who make the mistake, it is important as parents to learn how our actions made our children feel. Listening has so much power to heal. When a child can be expressive enough to share her feelings and thoughts, it gives way to openness and forgiveness. An apology from a parent can go an extremely long way. At the same time, it is also appropriate to have a boundary set for when feelings seem to go overboard or become counterproductive. If there is room for an honest assessment but also a boundary for proper guidance, forgiveness can make its way into hearts.

As parents, there will be a lot of opportunities for growth, for self-control, and for grace. Likewise, when a child does something wrong, it is just as important to walk through the process with them as well (and that often depends on the age of the child). The first several years of parenting seem to focus more on parental forgiveness, sleepless nights, and a lot of expended energy. We are then granted the opportunities to pay it forward!

What are some ways that you can remain more self-aware about listening? Where are some areas where a proper boundary needs to be set? What are some things that just need to be let go?

A Simple Prayer

Jesus, give me ears to listen and wisdom to share.
Let me always have a heart of humility so that forgiveness
can reign in me as a lifestyle.

Day 38

You will tell his people how to be saved through the forgiveness of their sins.
Luke 1:77

Forgiveness responds, not reacts. When in doubt, it is good to take a quiet stance. Refuse to give back frustration in words, in haste, or in argument. Settle yourself before trying to engage in a difficult situation. It is often best to give time for inside work before addressing anything that feels out of your control. The responsibility of a mother is often high, but it can be handled with grace. There are many times where we will feel overwhelmed, overextended, and stretched beyond our capacity. It is the nature of the job! But before reacting, even if we have the right to react, it is always more gratifying to choose a minute to breathe, reset our focus, and then respond. Forgiveness is often as simple as that. We choose not to destructively react even though we could. We remember that our children are still learning, and they learn by our example. Many times we are frustrated not because they have done anything wrong but simply because it takes a lot of energy to teach all the time. When we can focus on reality, it helps us take daily hiccups into a proper perspective.

What are your most triggering situations with your children? When they do not listen? When they get messy? Temper tantrums? Try taking a quiet stance before reacting in any of these situations. Find a great online parenting resource to help you process through healthy guidelines for these triggering circumstances. Try to understand, breathe, and respond with love.

A Simple Prayer

Jesus, please grant me the patience I need to be a loving parent.
Help me to pause and to listen before I make a response.
Help me to always choose love.

Day 39

Since I know, my God, that you examine the mind and take delight in honesty,
I have freely given all these things with the highest of motives.
1 Chronicles 29:17a

Honesty is the key to forgiveness! Parenting thrives on authenticity and communication. When we are honest with our feelings in a healthy manner, our kids will also be honest with theirs. One of the most important tools for mothering is communication. When we learn how to listen and how to respond with one another, there is no obstacle or situation that cannot be supported and transformed into an opportunity for growth. Stress is most often caused because of a lack of expression. When we give expression to our hurt or frustration, we honor ourselves. We release what is trapped inside. And when we can share this with our children, they get to see a healthy example of authentic self-care. They reflect our example. We set the stage for them to be able to have their own process while also assuring them we will be there for support. Authentic communication is the key to true forgiveness and healthy interactions as a family.

Practice listening. Practice self-awareness and honesty. Practice expressing yourself in a healthy way. This can start privately by keeping a journal or talking with an adult friend, or even talking with your child. Look for ways to learn how to communicate effectively. It will grow your relationship for years to come!

A Simple Prayer

Jesus, give me the courage to be honest with myself.
Help me to foster my authenticity though it may seem new and
uncomfortable. Help me to lead with forgiveness.

Day 40

*Jesus called the children to him and said, "Let the little children come to me,
and do not hinder them, for the kingdom of God belongs to such as these. Truly
I tell you, anyone who will not receive the kingdom of God like a little child
will never enter it."*
Luke 18:16-17 NIV

We made it! A journey through identity, expectations, grief, self-care, comparison, self-acceptance, presence, and forgiveness all intertwined in the life of a mother. There is so much to be grateful for as we embark on this adventure of parenting, loving, and giving. It truly is a gift; it comes with great challenges and great rewards. There really is nothing else like it. As life continues to propel forward, remember that the little things are the big things—and there is joy to be found in it all! Take a moment today to celebrate. You are a great mother; you took time out to experience this journey because you care. You care about the well-being of yourself and of your family. Yes, there will be mistakes. But there will also be honest conversation, nurturing of wounds, a lot of forgiveness, and even more joy.

Take a few minutes to write a gratitude list. During the course of the day, continue to add all the things you are thankful for to your list. At the end of the day, read them out loud. This is the beginning of a newfound season of joy! And always remember that motherhood is a journey, so repeat this devotional as often as you want. Each season will carry its own lessons, and you can weave these forty days into your life again and again as you plunge through new heights and new depths as a mother.

So when in doubt, just *repeat*!

A Simple Prayer

*Thank You, Jesus! I am grateful for your nurture, care, and grace over my life.
Help me to be the best mother I can be, to continually accept Your
mercies with each new morning, and to live a life to the
fullest for Your glory, myself, and my family.*

the joy of the Lord is my strength

nehemiah 8:10

You teach me the way of life. In Your presence is total celebration. Beautiful things are always in your right hand.

Psalm 16:11